MW01155868

Lerner SPORTS

GREATEST OF ALL TIME PLAYERS

G.O.A.T. BASEBALL OUTFIELDERS

Alexander Lowe

Lerner Publications ◆ Minneapolis

Lerner Publications Company
An imprint of Lerner Publishing Group, Inc.
241 First Avenue North
Minneapolis, MN 55401 USA

For reading levels and more information, look up this title at www.lernerbooks.com.

Main body text set in Aptifer Sans LT Pro.
Typeface provided by Linotype AG.

Library of Congress Cataloging-in-Publication Data
Names: Lowe, Alexander, author.
Title: G.O.A.T. baseball outfielders / Alexander Lowe.
Other titles: Greatest of all time baseball outfielders
Description: Minneapolis : Lerner Publications, [2022] | Series: Greatest of All Time Players (Lerner Sports) | Includes bibliographical references and index. | Audience: Ages 7–11 | Audience: Grades 4–6 | Summary: "Baseball boasts some of the world's best athletes. Learn how the top outfielders carried their teams to victory. Then make your own list of the greatest outfielders in MLB history!"—Provided by publisher.
Identifiers: LCCN 2021022668 (print) | LCCN 2021022669 (ebook) | ISBN 9781728441108 (library binding) | ISBN 9781728448411 (paperback) | ISBN 9781728444741 (ebook)
Subjects: LCSH: Outfielders (Baseball)—United States—Juvenile literature. | Outfielders (Baseball)—Rating of—United States—Juvenile literature. | Baseball—United States—History—Juvenile literature. | Baseball—United States—Statistics—Juvenile literature.
Classification: LCC GV865.A1 L67 2022 (print) | LCC GV865.A1 (ebook) | DDC 796.357/25—dc23

LC record available at https://lccn.loc.gov/2021022668
LC ebook record available at https://lccn.loc.gov/2021022669

Manufactured in the United States of America
2-1008772-49724-8/9/2022

TABLE OF CONTENTS

Nicknamed the Say Hey Kid for the friendly greeting he gave everyone he met, Willie Mays had nearly 200 career assists (throws that led to outs).

THE BEST OUTFIELDERS IN BASEBALL HISTORY

The New York Giants faced off against the Cleveland Indians in Game 1 of the 1954 World Series. The game was tied in the top of the eighth inning. Vic Wertz hit a ball deep to the outfield. The ball flew around 420 feet (128 m) to center field. In most stadiums, the hit would have been a home run. But the Giants' stadium was bigger than most. There was room for the ball to drop.

FACTS AT A GLANCE

- » BABE RUTH WAS ALSO A PITCHER BEFORE HE SWITCHED TO THE OUTFIELD.
- » HANK AARON HOLDS THE RECORD FOR THE MOST ALL-STAR GAME APPEARANCES.
- » THE TOP THREE CAREER HOME RUN LEADERS WERE ALL OUTFIELDERS: BARRY BONDS, HANK AARON, AND BABE RUTH.
- » KEN GRIFFEY JR. HIT A HOME RUN IN THE FINAL GAME PLAYED AT THE KINGDOME IN SEATTLE, WASHINGTON.

Giants center fielder Willie Mays was close to the infield expecting Wertz to hit a weak fly ball. But the ball soared deep into the outfield. Mays put his head down and sprinted back toward the wall. Just before the ball hit the ground, Mays stuck his mitt out to make the incredible catch. He saved the game for his team.

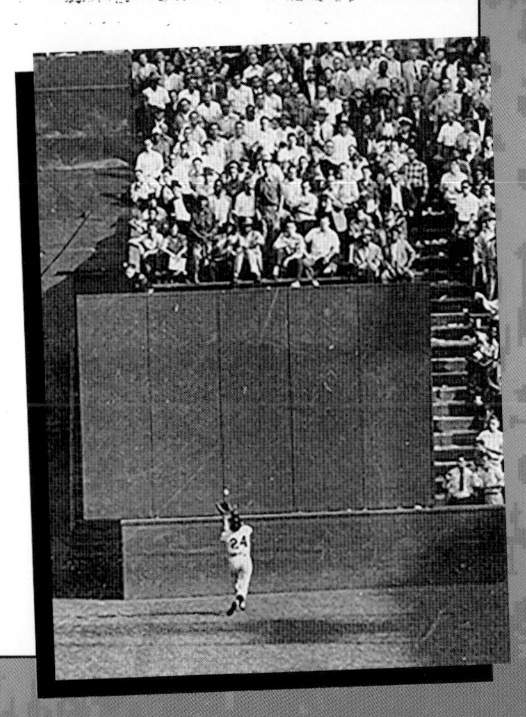

Baseball outfielders are great defenders. The three outfield positions are left field, center field, and right field. The players who play these positions must cover more than three-quarters of the baseball field. Outfielders are fast runners and need to know where the ball is going. They also need strong arms to make throws that are over 300 feet (91 m).

Outfielders play in the grass beyond the infield. They are responsible for the largest part of the playing field during a game.

Ken Griffey Jr. could do it all. He was a great hitter, a fast runner, and an outstanding defensive player.

Outfielders are very important on offense as well. Some of the best power hitters in baseball history have been outfielders. Many of the top base stealers have also played outfield. The best outfielders have been some of the greatest of all time, or the G.O.A.T.!

No. 10 KEN GRIFFEY JR.

Fans loved watching Ken Griffey Jr. play. The Kid became famous for his relaxed style and trademark smile. Griffey was so popular that a video game was named after him.

Griffey is best known for his time with the Seattle Mariners. He is still their all-time team leader in home runs. He hit a home run in the final game ever played in the Kingdome, Seattle's long-time stadium. He ended his career with 630 home runs, which ranks seventh on the Major League Baseball (MLB) all-time list.

Griffey was a five-tool player. He could run, hit for average, hit for power, field, and throw. Few players in MLB history could match Griffey's skills at the plate and in the field.

KEN GRIFFEY JR. STATS

Batting Average	.284
Hits	2,781
Home Runs	630
RBIs	1,836

No. 9 TED WILLIAMS

Many say Ted Williams is the greatest hitter ever. His .482 on-base percentage is the best in history. He led the American League (AL) in batting average six times and in home runs four times.

In 1941, Williams had a .406 batting average. Since then, no hitter has come close to matching that average for a full season. Williams was obsessed with the art of hitting. He said he wanted to be the greatest hitter who ever lived. He worked tirelessly to reach that goal.

Williams's stats could have been even better. However, World War II (1939–1945) interrupted his career. Williams left baseball for three years to serve in the US Navy. He returned to MLB in 1946 and continued to play at a high level. That year, he smacked 38 home runs and won the AL Most Valuable Player (MVP) award for the first time.

TED WILLIAMS STATS

Batting Average	.344
Hits	2,654
Home Runs	521
RBIs	1,839

No. 8 ICHIRO SUZUKI

Ichiro Suzuki was already a star in Japan when he joined MLB in 2001. The right fielder was ready to make an impact from day one. Ichiro was only the second player in MLB history to win both the Rookie of the Year and MVP awards in the same season.

Ichiro did not slow down after his incredible rookie year. He had over 200 hits in ten straight seasons. He led the AL in hits seven of those years. Ichiro's combined hits in Japan and MLB total 4,367.

Ichiro's greatness was not limited to hitting. He won ten Gold Gloves. This award is presented to the best defensive player at each position. His speed helped him track down balls other defenders couldn't reach. His strong arm meant that base runners had to think twice before going for an extra base when the ball was hit to right field.

ICHIRO SUZUKI STATS

Batting Average	.311
MLB Hits	3,089
Home Runs	117
RBIs	780

No. 7 MICKEY MANTLE

The New York Yankees have had a long list of great players. In the 1950s, no one was more popular than Mickey Mantle. He was voted to play in the All-Star Game in 16 of his 18 seasons. He led the Yankees to seven World Series titles. He won the MVP award three times. Two of those were back-to-back in 1956 and 1957.

Mantle was known for his speed in the outfield and his power at the plate. The Yankees were the first team to measure home run distances. They started doing this to track the long shots from Mantle. His swing was designed to hit the ball with power every time he batted. Mantle's swing inspired whole generations of future players.

In his rookie season in 1951, Mantle injured his knee in Game 2 of the World Series. He had many injuries during his 18-year career. But Mantle still earned his spot as one of the G.O.A.T.

MICKEY MANTLE STATS

Batting Average	.298
Hits	2,415
Home Runs	536
RBIs	1,509

No. 6 MIKE TROUT

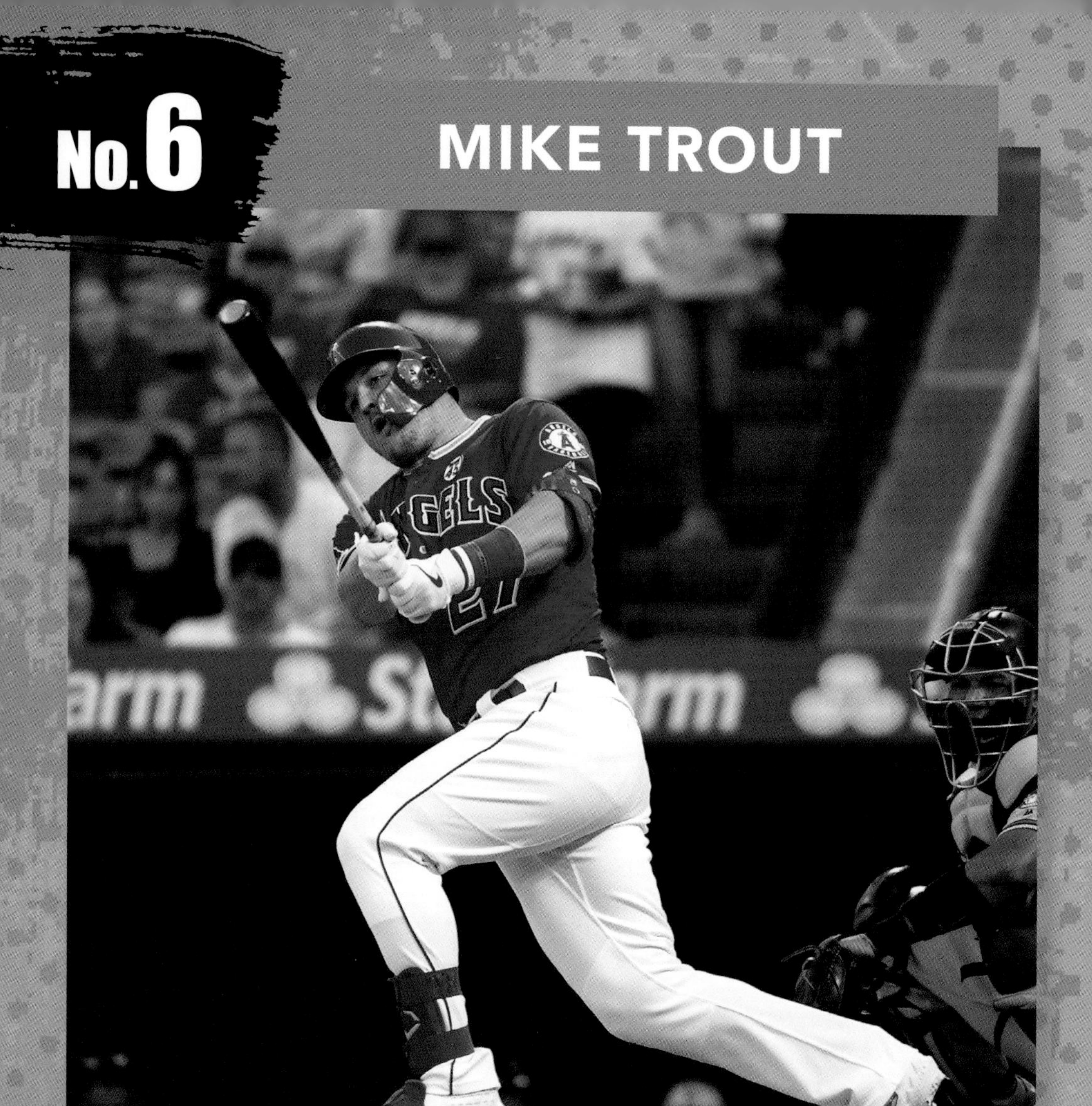

Mike Trout is one of the best players in MLB. By the time his career ends, he may end up being the G.O.A.T. From the start of his career, Trout has been an elite player. He has finished in the top five of MVP voting in every one of his full seasons.

Wins above replacement, or WAR, is a stat that tracks a player's overall value. It determines how many wins a player is worth. Trout had a higher WAR through age 20 than any player in history. He has already led the AL in WAR five times.

Trout has no weaknesses. He tracks down fly balls with ease. At the plate, he hits for both power and average. Trout has more than 200 stolen bases in his career. He has been an All-Star in every full season he has played. No current player can compare with Trout's greatness.

MIKE TROUT STATS

Batting Average	.305
Hits	1,419
Home Runs	310
RBIs	816

No. 5 TY COBB

Ty Cobb is one of the greatest hitters to ever live. Not only did he hit over .400 in three different seasons with the Detroit Tigers, but he also has the highest career batting average in MLB history.

Cobb was especially known for his great baserunning. Despite retiring almost 100 years ago, Cobb still ranks fourth all time in stolen bases. Cobb is also the only player to lead the league in homers without hitting a ball over the fence. He had an incredible nine inside-the-park home runs in one season.

When he retired, Cobb had set 90 MLB records. Some still stand today. He has the record for highest career batting average (.367). He won the AL batting title 12 times, more than any other player. There is no debating Cobb's greatness.

TY COBB STATS

Batting Average	.367
Hits	4,189
Home Runs	117
RBIs	1,944

No. 4 HANK AARON

Hammerin' Hank Aaron retired as the all-time MLB leader in home runs. He broke a record that had stood for more than 30 years. Aaron is still ranked second on MLB's all-time home run list behind Barry Bonds.

Aaron's home run record was a milestone for racial equality in baseball. For more than 50 years, Black athletes were not allowed to play in MLB. That ended in 1947 when Jackie Robinson began playing for the Brooklyn Dodgers. Aaron joined the league in 1954 and became MLB's home run champion in 1974.

Aaron is remembered as the Home Run King, but he was much more than that. He had more than 3,000 hits that were not home runs. He still holds the career RBI record. Aaron made history by being named an All-Star for an incredible 21 seasons in a row.

HANK AARON STATS

Batting Average	.305
Hits	3,771
Home Runs	755
RBIs	2,297

No. 3 BARRY BONDS

Barry Bonds had it all. Early in his career, he was a great defender. He won five Gold Gloves before he turned 30. He also ran fast, stealing 52 bases in a single season. Bonds had a powerful swing. He ended his MLB career as the league's all-time home run champion.

Bonds was at his best in 2001. He set a new record by hitting 73 home runs. Opposing pitchers were afraid to face Bonds. He recorded 688 intentional walks in his career. Sometimes he was even intentionally walked with the bases loaded. The opposing team preferred to give up one run than the four that Bonds could drive in with a home run.

Bonds and other players from his era may have used steroids to improve their performances. Bonds says that he never knowingly took them. No one is sure exactly how much steroids may have helped Bonds as he dominated the league during his career.

BARRY BONDS STATS

Batting Average	.298
Hits	2,935
Home Runs	762
RBIs	1,996

No. 2 BABE RUTH

Babe Ruth may be the most famous baseball player ever. The Great Bambino was a feared power hitter. His skill and strength with a bat changed the game forever.

Ruth led MLB in home runs 12 times. In 1927, he set a new record by blasting 60 homers. His most famous home run came in 1932. Ruth pointed to the center field fence and then smacked the next pitch over it. He retired after the 1935 season as the career home run leader.

Ruth was not just a great hitter. He was also a talented pitcher. He pitched in 163 games in his career. But his best years were played as an outfielder, when he became the most dominant hitter in the league.

BABE RUTH STATS

Batting Average	.342
Hits	2,873
Home Runs	714
RBIs	2,214

No. 1 WILLIE MAYS

Willie Mays is the greatest all-around player that baseball has ever seen. His combination of offense and defense is unmatched. He had many great individual seasons in his 22-year career. He also logged some of the best career numbers in MLB history.

Mays was best known for his incredible defense. People still talk about his most famous catch. Mays ran nearly 200 feet (61 m) to center field and caught the ball over his shoulder. Plays like that happened all the time for Mays. He won the Gold Glove 12 straight years.

Mays was also one of the finest hitters to ever play the game. He ended his career with 660 home runs, which ranked third when he retired in 1973. He led the league in WAR 10 times. At bat and in the field, Mays proved that he was the G.O.A.T.

WILLIE MAYS STATS

Batting Average	.302
Hits	3,283
Home Runs	660
RBIs	1,903

EVEN MORE G.O.A.T.

There have been many other great players who played in the outfield. Choosing the G.O.A.T. is a tough task. Here are 10 more players who nearly made the top-10 list.

No. 11	TRIS SPEAKER
No. 12	RICKEY HENDERSON
No. 13	STAN MUSIAL
No. 14	FRANK ROBINSON
No. 15	ANDRUW JONES
No. 16	ROBERTO CLEMENTE
No. 17	JOE DIMAGGIO
No. 18	AL KALINE
No. 19	VLADIMIR GUERRERO
No. 20	TONY GWYNN

YOUR G.O.A.T.

It's your turn to make a G.O.A.T. list about baseball outfielders. Start by doing research. Consider the rankings in this book. Then check out the Learn More section on page 31. Explore the books and websites to learn more about baseball players of the past and present.

You can search online for more information about great players too. Check with a librarian, who may have other resources for you. You might even try reaching out to baseball teams or players to see what they think.

Once you're ready, make your list of the greatest outfielders of all time. Then ask people you know to make G.O.A.T. lists and compare them. Do you have players no one else listed? Are you missing anybody your friends think is important? Talk it over, and try to convince them that your list is the G.O.A.T.!

GLOSSARY

batting average: a stat found by dividing the number of times at bat into the number of base hits

infield: the area of a baseball field enclosed by the three bases and home plate

intentional walk: an advance to first base awarded to a baseball player by the opposing team to prevent the player from swinging the bat

milestone: an important point in progress

on-base percentage: a stat that indicates how often a batter reaches base by a hit, a walk, or being hit by a pitch

RBI: a run in baseball that is driven in by a batter

rookie: a first-year player

steroid: a performance-enhancing drug

stolen base: when a runner advances a base without the ball being hit

WAR: wins above replacement, a statistic that tracks how valuable a player is compared to an average player

LEARN MORE

Baseball Hall of Fame
https://baseballhall.org/

Burrell, Dean. *Baseball Biographies for Kids: The Greatest Players from the 1960s to Today.* Emeryville, CA: Rockridge Press, 2021.

Fishman, Jon M. *Baseball's G.O.A.T.: Babe Ruth, Mike Trout, and More.* Minneapolis: Lerner Publications, 2020.

Hank Aaron Biography
https://mrnussbaum.com/hank-aaron-biography

Leed, Percy. *Hank Aaron: Home Run Hammer.* Minneapolis: Lerner Publications, 2022.

MLB: Kids Activities Page
https://www.mlb.com/fans/kids/activities

INDEX

PHOTO ACKNOWLEDGMENTS

Image credits: Christof Koepsel/Staff/pngimg.com, p.3; Alamy, p.4; Gareth Owen/Wikimedia, p.5; Joseph Sohm/Shutterstock, p.6; Christian Petersen/Staff/Getty Images, p.7; Ezra Shaw/Staff/Getty Images, p.8; Stephen Dunn/Staff/Getty Images, p.9; Hulton Archive/Stringer/Getty Images, p.10; Alon Alexander/Alamy, p.11; Masterpress/Stringer/Getty Images, p.12; Jonathan Daniel/Stringer/Getty Images, p.13; Frederic Lewis/Staff/Getty Images, p.14; Hulton Archive/Stringer/Getty Images, p.15; Kevork Djansezian/Stringer/Getty Images, p.16; John McCoy/Stringer/Getty Images, p.17; Archive World/Alamy, p.18; Hulton Archive/Stringer/Getty Images, p.19; Everett Collection Historical/Alamy, p.20; BUD SKINNER/KRT/Newscom, p.21; Jed Jacobsohn/Staff/Getty Images, 22; Jonathan Daniel/Staff/Getty Images, p.23; Topical Press Agency/Stringer/Getty Images, p.24; Ewing Galloway/Newscom, p.25; Hulton Archive/Stringer/Getty Images, p.26; Archive Photos/Stringer/Getty Images, p.27; Nadezhda Shpiiakina/Shutterstock, Background;

Cover: Otto Greule Jr/Stringer/Getty Images; Drew Hallowell/Stringer/Getty Images; Gergory Shamus/Staff/Getty Images; Nadezhda Shpiiankina/Shutterstock